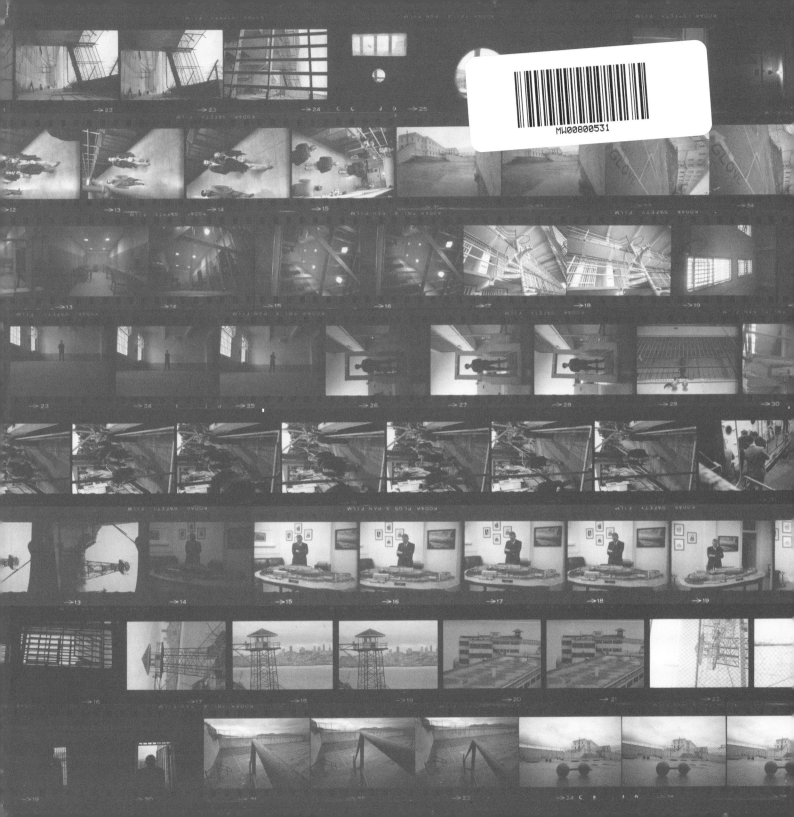

ALCATRAZ

THE LAST DAY

ALCATRAZ
THE LAST DAY

Photographs by Leigh Wiener

Introduction by Carl Nolte

Golden Gate National Parks Conservancy
San Francisco, California

ISBN 978-1-932519-13-6
Library of Congress Control Number: 2011925118

Art Direction: Robert Lieber
Design: Alvaro Villanueva
Editor: Susan Tasaki
Production: Sarah Lau
Assistance: John Moran, John Cantwell

PARKS FOR ALL FOREVER™

The Golden Gate National Parks Conservancy is the nonprofit
membership organization created to preserve the Golden Gate
National Parks, enhance the experiences of park visitors, and build
a community dedicated to conserving the parks for the future.

Printed and bound in Hong Kong

Sources Referenced

Albright, Jim. *Last Guard Out*. Bloomington, IN:
Author House, 2008.

Carceral, K. C. (pseud.); T. J. Bernard, L. F. Alarid, B.
Birkle, and A. Birkle, eds. *Behind a Convict's Eyes*.
Belmont, CA: Wadsworth, 2004.

Grassick, Mary. "Alcatraz Island: Main Prison Building,"
Historic Furnishings Report. Harpers Ferry, WV:
Harpers Ferry Center, National Park Service, 2005.

Gregory, George. *Alcatraz Screw: My Years as
a Guard in America's Most Notorious Prison*.
Columbia: University of Missouri Press, 2008.

Heaney, Frank. *Inside the Walls of Alcatraz*. Self-
published, 1987.

Lageson, Ernest, Sr. and Jr. *Guarding the Rock: A
Father and Son Remember Alcatraz*. San Francisco:
Golden Gate National Parks Conservancy, 2008.

Mahoney, Patrick. *My Dirty, Wonderful Job*. San
Francisco: Golden Gate National Parks Conservancy
(forthcoming).

Newspaper quotes: http://news.google.com/
archivesearch

Oral histories, GGNRA/Park Archives and Records
Center: Philip Bergen and Patrick Mahoney.

Quillen, Jim. *Alcatraz from Inside*. San Francisco:
Golden Gate National Parks Conservancy, 1991.

Thompson, Erwin N. "The Rock: A History of Alcatraz
Island, 1847–1972," Historic Resources Study. Denver:
Denver Service Center, National Park Service, 1979.

CONTENTS

FOREWORD

When I was a child, my father—Los Angeles-based photographer, filmmaker, and producer Leigh Wiener—would sometimes take me out of school so I could go with him on quick trips north to San Francisco. On one of those occasions, I remember looking at Alcatraz Island from the city shoreline and wondering what it was like. At the time, it was still off-limits, so visiting it in order to satisfy my interest, which was no doubt fueled by things I'd heard and read about the place, wasn't an option.

Years later, while inventorying my father's archive of proof sheets and negatives, I was astonished to discover a treasure trove of more than 300 images of Alcatraz, shot on March 21, 1963, the day the prison closed. They had been taken on assignment for *Life*, one of his long-term clients (over the years, he had 144 assignments from the magazine).

Though he had once mentioned it to me, he didn't go into detail, and I'd forgotten about it. March 1963 was a busy month for him; on his calendar were photo sessions with Judy Garland, Mickey Rooney, and movie moguls Jack Warner and Daryl Zanuck.

Most of my friends' fathers went to work carrying briefcases. Mine carried cameras—usually Nikon Fs and Leicas that could stand quite a bit of abuse on location—and a variety of lenses. Depending on the requirements of the job, he sometimes loaded one camera with black-and-white film and another with color. He was also good at improvising in order to get the shot he wanted.

During my father's decades-long career as a photojournalist and photographer, he captured many of our country's cultural and political icons on film. In the 1960s alone, he photographed California governor Pat Brown, artist Marc Chagall, jazz drummer Chico Hamilton, Richard Nixon, John and Robert Kennedy, baseball great Sandy Koufax, and ballet dancer extraordinaire Rudolf Nureyev, among many others. As these images accumulated, he kept them first in filing cabinets in his Hollywood office, then in a vault in his studio. When he retired in the early '80s, he had a vault built beneath his house in the Hollywood Hills to store the negatives and proof sheets that made up his life's work.

When he died in 1993, I became the caretaker of his photographic legacy. It took me eighteen months to catalog the thousands of images, which I then had moved into a secure and climate-controlled storage facility for safekeeping.

On a 2009 trip to San Francisco, I finally indulged my curiosity and took the ferry to Alcatraz, seeing the island up close for the first time. This connection between a place and my father's work inspired me to contact National Park Service interpreters and archivists to let them know about the Alcatraz photos. From that contact, this book was born.

—*Devik Wiener, Los Angeles, California*

WARNING
KEEP OFF

PERSONS ATTEMPTING
TO COME INSIDE BUOYS
WITHOUT PERMISSION
DO SO AT THEIR PERIL

ALCATRAZ: NO GOOD FOR NOBODY
by Carl Nolte

For years, rumors had swirled like fog around Alcatraz, the military prison island in the middle of San Francisco Bay. It was a closed world, an island where dangerous men were locked up.

In the 1930s, the rumors became fact. Alcatraz, the old military post turned army disciplinary barracks, was to become America's most feared federal prison. The army, which found the prison difficult to maintain, was getting ready to turn the island over to a different agency: the civilian Bureau of Prisons (BOP), an arm of the Department of Justice.

During the 1920s, the United States was rocked by a crime wave heated up by Prohibition. Every town, it seemed, had its speakeasy or roadhouse where illegal liquor was available, much of it supplied by criminals. Fast boats and ships—the so-called "rum runners"—came down from Canada bringing liquor, and business was brisk. Locally, Sausalito, a small town along the waterfront just north of Alcatraz Island, was known to be "wide-open," a place where it wasn't too hard to find a speakeasy stocked with alcohol made in backyard stills or brought in by the rum runners.

Then, in the 1930s, as the country sank into the Great Depression, criminals became folk heroes. Men like John Dillinger and "Baby Face" Nelson, couples like Bonnie and Clyde, bank robbers and kidnappers who defied the law and sometimes killed people while doing it, captured the American public's imagination, and stories about them and their activities dominated the news. To combat this disturbing trend, the government organized special crime-fighting units, whose members called themselves G Men (a term that eventually became associated with FBI agents). This 1930s war on crime resulted in the arrests of many high-profile prisoners—among them, Al "Scarface" Capone.

By 1933, with the fight against organized crime in full swing, the federal government had that decided a new "super prison" was needed. And then, in what seemed to be a masterpiece of stagecraft, it determined that Alcatraz, a rock surrounded by the cold waters of San Francisco Bay, was the ideal place.

In fact, the government seemed to think that San Francisco should be honored to have a prison in the bay. "In brief, it seems to the Department of Justice that there is

> *The establishment by the Department of Justice of a Federal Prison at Alcatraz Island is a necessary part of the Government's campaign against predatory crime....*
>
> *It will not be a Devil's Island. It will be an integral part of the Federal Prison System, operated in conformity with advanced ideas of penology and with the ultimate object in view of protecting all our communities ... it will house a mere handful of men. The Department of Justice pledges itself to take every possible precaution to prevent escapes.*
>
> —Memorandum, Department of Justice
> November 6, 1933

1

presented a splendid opportunity for the citizens of San Francisco to cooperate in a patriotic and public spirited manner in the Government's campaign against the criminal," according to the DOJ memo.

The army pulled out and the first federal prisoners arrived in 1934. Over the years, some of the most famous criminals in the world were kept on Alcatraz—Al Capone; "Creepy" Karpis, the government's official Public Enemy Number One; "Machine Gun" Kelly; "Doc" Barker; and Robert Stroud, the famous Birdman. In fact, the government used Alcatraz as a dumping ground for problem prisoners, not just hard cases and desperate men. It was known as the Rock, a name intended to strike fear into the dark hearts of criminals. As inmate Henry Young testified during his trial for the 1940 murder of a fellow convict, Deputy Warden E. J. Miller told him, "Alcatraz is not a penitentiary. Alcatraz is Alcatraz."

But the world that created grim places like USP Alcatraz

Alcatraz Prison Also a Fortress—On its lonely rock, it is as secure as man and nature are able to make it.

—*New York Times*,
September 2, 1934

We strongly urge elimination Alcatraz Penitentiary in San Francisco Bay as menace to population in light of recent riots. We suggesting [sic] that it be moved to some isolated point rather than be continued in a center of population. Request your immediate comment via wire and whether you will support such move.

—Telegram to Hon. William F. Knowland, Washington, D.C., from Josh Eppinger, City Editor, *San Francisco Examiner*, May 8, 1946

began to change, and by 1960, the torch had been passed to a new generation of Americans, exemplified by the election of John F. Kennedy. The idea of a dead-end, escape-proof prison island seemed like something out of another age.

Attitudes had changed in San Francisco as well. When the federal prison was established in the mid-1930s, in the depths of the Depression, San Francisco had just gone through a huge and bloody waterfront strike. Times were tough. Any jobs, especially good government jobs at a prison, were welcome.

When Alcatraz opened, the only way to cross San Francisco Bay was by ferryboat. The Bay Bridge connecting San Francisco and Oakland opened in 1936, and the famous Golden Gate Bridge went into service in the spring of 1937.

Before that, all the ferryboats between San Francisco and Marin County to the north passed by Alcatraz; parents could point out the prison island to their children as a cautionary tale: "Look at that place, son. If you don't behave, you'll end up there." It was a chilling experience.

During World War II, San Francisco Bay became an enormous staging area for soldiers, sailors, and marines heading to the Pacific. Millions of men on their way to the war passed that grim island.

When the war was over and the prisoners rioted in 1946, the marines were called in to retake the island. Citizens in San Francisco gathered on the Marina Green in the city to watch the gunfire. It was a surreal scene.

As time went on, Alcatraz came to be considered as a relic, an institution that had outlived its purpose, especially once the public began to realize that it was not anywhere near as escape-proof as the government wanted them to believe.

In the post-war era, San Francisco grew into a world-class city, famous for its beauty. During the 1950s, the Beats, a whole generation of poets and writers, came to North Beach, and San Francisco's opera and symphony flourished. The nightclub scene along Broadway and Columbus was always jumping, and the city had jazz and a lively night life. It was both hot and very cool.

And at the end of night, walking the streets on the northern edge of the city, one could still see the brightly lit prison island, surrounded by the black water of the bay.

By the '60s, the city was prosperous. Woody Allen played in the city's clubs, and Barbra Streisand got her first big break here. You could still buy a nice house on Potrero Hill for $19,000 (it would be worth a cool million now), or a new Rambler V-8 for $3,000. Businessmen could outfit themselves in an Edward Hawk sharkskin suit for $79.50; newspaper ads showed handsome men dressed to the nines at work, while secretaries looked on admiringly, ready to take dictation.

Reporter J. Campbell Bruce wrote a book about the place—*Escape from Alcatraz*—though he was hindered by the fact that the BOP wouldn't allow him access to the prison's official records. But according to Bruce, by 1962, an accountant serving time for tax evasion, a man doing time for stealing a pig, another prisoner whose offense was stealing two cases of cigarettes, and a convict in for assault and a $1.50 robbery were rubbing shoulders on the Rock.

By then, rumors were once again circulating that the island prison might be closed. Then in March 1961, BOP director James Bennett threw cold water on the idea. Alcatraz warden Paul Madigan said he'd checked out the rumors with his boss. "Abandoning Alcatraz is the farthest thing from Bennett's mind," he said.

Still, there was unease about the prison. In April 1961, California State Senator J. Eugene McAteer, a powerful figure in the city, wrote to Attorney General Robert Kennedy to urge that USP Alcatraz be abandoned. He called it a conspicuous eyesore, expensive to operate, and obsolete.

About a year later, a House of Representatives subcommittee met in a closed-door session to hear some grim news from Bennett, who only the year before had told the Alcatraz warden that closing the prison was the furthest thing from his mind. This time, he told the congressmen that the concrete was chipping, the steel was rusting, and the prison was crumbling. It would cost $4 million to repair it, Bennett said. Unless they received an appropriation, the Bureau of Prisons would have to abandon Alcatraz.

Olin Blackwell, the Rock's new warden, stood up for his prison. "The fear of being sent to Alcatraz keeps some men in line," he said.

Has Alcatraz outlived its usefulness? Fewer prisoners than ever before are now being held in the escape-proof Federal prison in San Francisco Bay, and it's very expensive to operate—$8 a day to maintain each desperate guest.

—*Oakland Tribune*, May 12, 1949

U.S. May Close Alcatraz— Prison director tells of plan to build new institution

—*New York Times*, April 11, 1955

Island model in the Warden's office.

But the tide had begun to turn against the idea of a place as fearsome as Alcatraz. Allan Temko, an architectural critic for the *San Francisco Chronicle* who would later win the Pulitzer Prize, denounced the prison in the newspaper on February 12, 1962.

"Of all the excrescences which have been senselessly permitted to disfigure San Francisco Bay—perhaps the most magnificent natural resource of any metropolitan area in the world—the prison on Alcatraz Island belongs to a unique category of uncivilized ugliness," he wrote.

"This remnant of medieval penology has made us all its prisoners…. This brutal jail, a miniature local version of the *Ile du Diable*, has outlived any functional justification it may once have had, and is now literally falling into ruin."

The government, Temko wrote, should seize on its exorbitant maintenance and repair cost "as a golden opportunity to rid the bay of its worst eyesore."

The following month, California Lieutenant Governor Glenn Anderson agreed with this view. In a letter to Bennett, he called Alcatraz "a psychological and aesthetic disgrace. It is appalling that one of the most beautiful settings in the country should be defaced by this monument to human frailty."

Nonetheless, the prison still had supporters. Senator Edward Long (D-Missouri), chairman of the senate finance committee's subcommittee on prisons, toured the island and announced that Alcatraz still had value as a deterrent.

On June 11, 1962, not long after this announcement, Frank Morris and brothers John and Clarence Anglin managed to pick away at the crumbling walls of their cells, climb to the roof, and disappear. They were never seen again, but the escape from the supposedly escape-proof prison was a shock to the Bay Area.

San Francisco Mayor George Christopher, a powerful member of the state's Republican establishment, now added his voice to the call for closing the prison. He wanted a joint city/state/federal commission to plan a future for the island. His first idea was for a large statue, comparable to the Statue of Liberty in New York harbor. Or, he thought, perhaps some kind of tourist attraction, like the Tivoli Gardens in Copenhagen.

The next week, Congressman John Shelley (D-California), elected to the House of Representatives from San Francisco, told the House in a speech that Alcatraz was "a penological anachronism," and urged its abandonment. In its place, he suggested a statue of St. Francis of Assisi, the saint for whom the city is named. It would be "a monument of good, rather than evil," he said.

Even some prison guards felt Alcatraz had outlived its time. "The experiment of Alcatraz—with it severe hardships and deprivation—had become very controversial, almost an embarrassment to the 'modern society' of the time," Frank Heaney, a former correctional officer, wrote in his 1987 book, *Inside the Walls of Alcatraz*.

On June 23, 1962, Attorney General Robert Kennedy said the prison would probably be closed in the next year. Then, within six months, two more inmates managed to escape. One of them ended up clinging to a rock just off the Alcatraz shore, but the second man wound up on the rocks near Fort Point, just below the Golden Gate bridge and on the very doorstep of the city—wet, bedraggled, exhausted, but alive.

By the new year, Alcatraz was being phased out. At the end of February, Mickey Cohen, one of the last of the prison's high-profile mobsters, had been transferred, and only 64 inmates remained on the island. By the first week of March, more had been taken off the Rock; 34 were left.

On March 21, 1963, the first day of spring, the last prisoners—"27 pale, quiet men" the *San Francisco Chronicle* called them—were taken off the island. In that day's issue of the *Oakland Tribune*, reporters Mike Mealey and Bill Bancroft gave Bay Area readers more details: "Alcatraz of the past is dead. The closing was abrupt and final. The prisoners, dressed in new, dull prison garb for the occasion, were taken by boat in two trips from the island. Guards and their families—some on the island for as long as 20 years—went in a third crossing to San Francisco."

There were no speeches, no tears, no final ceremony. "This place is hell," said a bank robber as he boarded the *Warden Blackwell*, the prison launch. "Maybe they're sending me to heaven now."

It was left to Frank C. Weatherman, a gun smuggler and jail breaker and the last convict off the island, to deliver the epitaph for the Rock. "Alcatraz never was no good for nobody," he said.

Carl Nolte, a veteran editor and long-time reporter for the San Francisco Chronicle, *has taught journalism at San Francisco State University; been a visiting fellow at the University of California, Berkeley; and is the author of several books on San Francisco history.*

March 21, 1963

The United States Penitentiary Alcatraz launch pulled away from the dock at Fort Mason on its way to the island, as it had every morning for twenty-nine years. But this day was different.

On board were journalists, photographers, and newsreel cameramen from across the country and around the world, eager to document the end of an era as well as get a behind-the-scenes look at the notorious prison.

One of them, photographer Leigh Wiener, came up from Los Angeles on assignment for *Life* magazine. In the portfolio that follows—a conduit to the island's past—Wiener's intriguing, never-before-seen photographs capture that history-making day in all its energy and detail.

Journalists, photographers, and cameramen mingle with prison staff as they board the Alcatraz launch at the Fort Mason dock and make their way to the island.

*"I'm going to
miss the Rock."*

—Olin Blackwell,
last warden of Alcatraz

11

"*It would cost a lot of money to put it in tip-top shape, and we have serious doubts that spending that much money would be justified.*"

—James V. Bennett, Director, US Bureau of Prisons, July 1962

Left: **Model Industries Building**
Right: **New Industries Building**

Overshadowed by the dock guard tower, reporters and photographers catch a ride to the top of the island.

The million-dollar views of San Francisco were old news to the men in the pickup headed back to the dock for another load of photographers. The large white buildings below the roadway are apartments for correctional officers and their families. The apartments, built along the edge of the former military parade ground, were demolished in 1971.

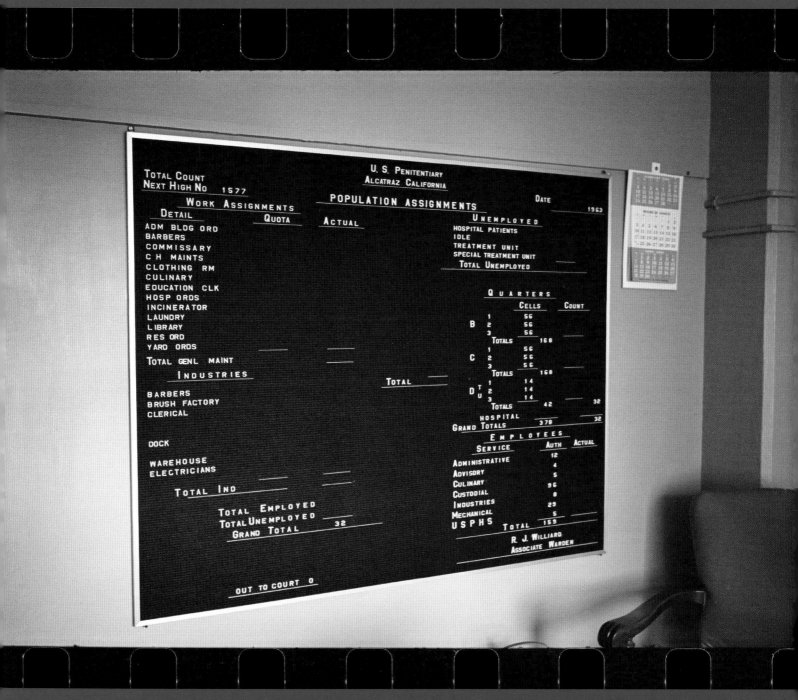

Administrative office

Leaving the Rock
by Jim Quillen, Inmate #AZ-586

The associate warden told me I was leaving Alcatraz. Ten years and one day of hell were coming to a close. Early the next evening, I was taken to the administrative office, where I was joined by three others being transferred. We were going to a new world.

We were handcuffed, shackled, and then chained together as a group. We were transported to the dock, where the prison launch waited to take us to Oakland.

In Oakland, we boarded a train. The rear car had been sectioned off and only prisoners and guards were permitted in this area. Once inside the car, the chain that held us together as a group was removed. Each of us, however, remained handcuffed and shackled to a partner. This made any movement difficult, especially the use of the restroom. At meals, our handcuffs were removed, but, as added security, our shackles were chained to the base of the seat. This eliminated any sudden movement or possible attack on the guards. Much of this close security was taken because of my long sentence and history of escapes.

The trip was uneventful and after many hours, we arrived in Steilacoom [Washington, site of USP McNeil Island].

Upon arriving at the prison, we were given a shower, a skin search, and a new issue of clothing. Again, the marking ink gave me a new identity. I was now #15874.

Jim Quillen served time at USP Alcatraz from 1942 to 1952; this account comes from his book, Alcatraz from Inside, *and describes his transfer from USP Alcatraz to USP McNeil. Though he left the island before the final closure, his experience mirrors that of the men who boarded the prison launch in March 1963, with one exception: in 1963, the convicts were transported by airplane rather than train.*

"*On their last day at Alcatraz, the inmates had breakfast, and then were subjected to a thorough strip search before being given their new clothes and chained with leg irons, belly chains, and handcuffs.*"

—Jim Albright,
Correctional Officer

Inmates normally entered and exited the prison through the basement. On March 21, for the first time, they passed through the prison's "front door."

"*The entrance at 'The Rock' is used to being locked shut. They had to prop the doors apart with a fire extinguisher and a cigarette-butt sandbox. Through here under a brooding sky, twenty-seven men shuffled out in leg irons to take a boat and a plane to other prisons.*"

—*Pittsburgh Press*, March 22, 1963

"*There was an air of ceremony. It centered on the departing prisoners; not on individuals, but on the group, all awesomely alike in fresh starched denims, white socks, shined shoes, and precise prison haircuts.*"

—*Pittsburgh Press*, March 22, 1963

"If you have ever tried to walk with leg irons, then you will understand when I say it is an art. You see, shackles are purposely made so one cannot walk normally. The first norm of the prison system I learned is the law of escorting officer in motion. Officers tend to *hurry only when a prisoner is in leg irons. Any other time, they're casual and slow moving."*

—Anonymous Inmate, quoted in *Behind a Convict's Eyes*

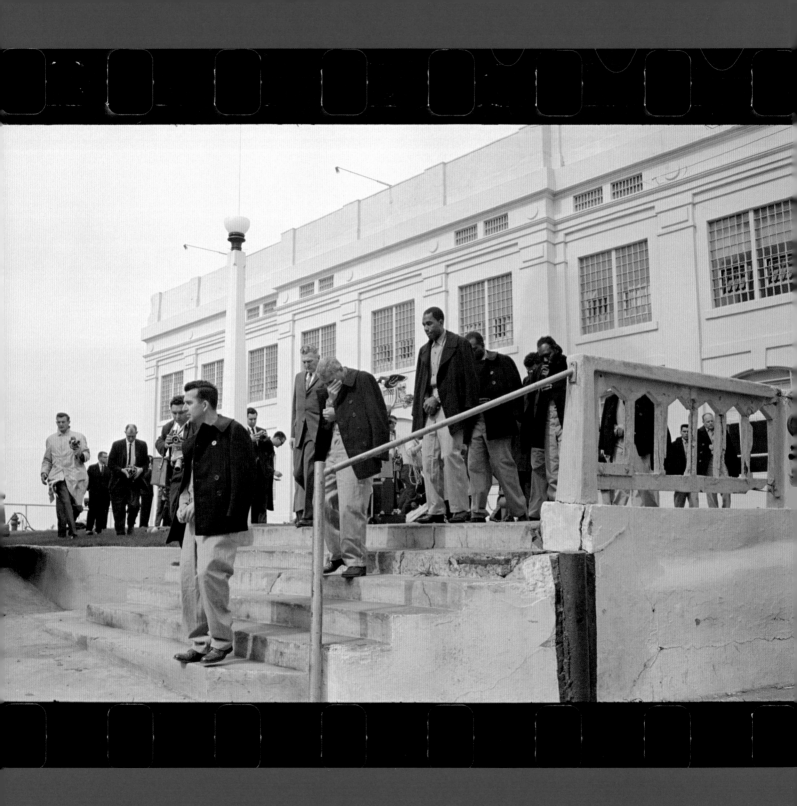

$\rightarrow$ 21

$\rightarrow$ 22

"*There comes a time in the lives of most men who are incarcerated when the light of reform flickers on in their minds. It comes seemingly out of nowhere and without any conscious volition of the inmate.... Unfortunately, in most, this flicker is lost and dies out in a short time.*"

—Rufus "Whitey" Franklin, Inmate #AZ-335

"The prison bus carried the men down to the dock in shifts. Before a new group boarded, one of the guards was assigned to search the bus for anything that could be used to pick a lock."

—Jim Albright, Correctional Officer

The photographer becomes part of his own photo; look carefully at the reflection in the lower portion of the upper left window of the bus door to see Leigh Wiener taking the shot.

Down the gangway from the dock to the launch.

The Last Boat Out

by Pat Mahoney, USP Alcatraz Correctional Officer and Boat Pilot

Someone at Alcatraz got in contact with the US Navy and the US Army and learned that the Armed Forces had an overstock of ten or twenty P-51–class vessels; we acquired two of them and converted them to passenger use. These were modern vessels, up to standard and equipped with radar. Warden Olin G. Blackwell insisted that one of the vessels be named after him; he named the other one *Warden Madigan* after his much-honored predecessor, Paul J. Madigan.

One day in 1963, when I was at the helm of the *Warden Madigan*, two Bureau of Prisons officials on their way to the penitentiary were on board. As usual, they rode with me on the bridge, and we talked. That's how I became the first correctional officer to know that Alcatraz was closing down.

They told us that Alcatraz was expensive to run. Compared to other prisons in the country, it cost three times as much per day to support a prisoner here. Half a century old and blasted by the marine climate, the facility was becoming dilapidated and difficult to maintain, and would be prohibitively costly to restore.

Alcatraz always attracted a lot of press interest. If a mishap occurred at any other penitentiary, it remained local news. But if it happened at Alcatraz, the world knew about it. Predictably, when news of Alcatraz's closure went worldwide, reporters came from around the globe to photograph and document the remaining inmates' parade from the facility to the launch.

By the time they came to cover the last boat taking prisoners out—which I piloted— there were fewer than thirty convicts left. Photos of these men exiting the penitentiary and filing onto the gangplank were plastered on front pages worldwide.

Pat Mahoney, who served as a correctional officer and boat pilot at USP Alcatraz from 1956 to 1963, narrates the Alcatraz Cellhouse audio tour.

"As the prison boat pulled away from the dock, Gordon J. Gronzo handed down his revolver, carbine, and 30-caliber rifle from the No. 1 gun tower. He was the last armed guard."

—San Francisco News Call Bulletin, March 21, 1963

Keys and locks became surplus once the inmates were gone.

"You will never *forget Alcatraz."*

—Jimmy Jimmerson,
Correctional Officer
(Quoted in *Alcatraz Screw*)

Left: **Warden Blackwell**
Right: **Unknown correctional officer**

"Every minute that you were inside the walls, it was dangerous, but you learned to live with that. This line of work has a high turnover.... It's a strange way of life ... and some men just can't get accustomed to it."

—Phil Bergen, Captain of the Guards

Tools of the trade: a metal detector (called a "snitch box" by inmates) and levers that operated the cell doors, which allowed all doors in a given row to be unlocked at the same time by a single correctional officer.

"*We got the people who couldn't be controlled. We did something no other institution—state or federal—was able to do at that time. We controlled these men, turned them around and returned them to other institutions in three to five years, and we did it in a decent, humane way.*"

—Phil Bergen, Captain of the Guards

"*Though we tried, no one totally understood the mental makeup of these captive humans and the reasons for their often-inhuman actions. When one entered the prison for a day's work, he entered an entirely different world.*"

—Ernest Lageson, Sr.,
Correctional Officer

→ 11

"You learned to walk wide around the corner of a cellblock. Someone not exactly interested in your good health could be waiting for you."

—George Gregory, Correctional Officer

All the cells were empty, all the inmates were gone. For the first time, correctional officers could relax inside the cellhouse.

Hospital therapy room.

Control Center key locker.

*Empty cell and empty chairs
in the visitors' room.*

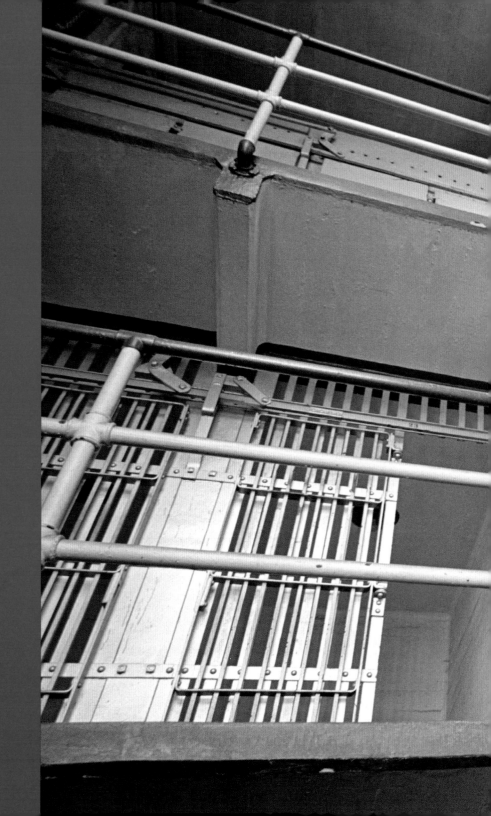

The first steps in Alcatraz Island's seventy-three-year history as a military prison were taken in 1861, when inmates from the Presidio joined those already in the island garrison's cells. Initially, prisoners were housed in one of the guardhouse casemates, then in a series of wooden buildings, and finally, in the massive concrete structure that crowns the island today.

USP Alcatraz's original inmates were the thirty-two bedraggled convicts the army had left behind when they officially vacated the island on June 19, 1934. Cellblock A, with its flat, soft-steel bars and circular staircase, looks much as it did during the military prison period. When the Bureau of Prisons upgraded security in the cellhouse, this block was left as is; the cells were used for storage and as meeting places for inmates and their attorneys.

Abandoned exercise equipment in the recreation yard.

"The inmates continued down another flight of stairs to the recreation area. Here they lined up along the painted lines on the pavement that designated the various shop details. The men in each shop were then counted and checked against a roster."

—Jim Quillen, Inmate #AZ-586

Agave crowd the walkway railing on the island's northwest side.

"I hated working the towers. God, it was monotonous, particularly the midnight-to-8 AM shift. It was always bitter cold, with chilling winds every night."

—Frank Heaney, Correctional Officer

"*Manning the towers was not just demanding, but stressful. It required vigilance and alertness to what was immediately in view and what trouble might be brewing ... especially around the outside perimeter of the prison.*"

—Jim Albright, Correctional Officer

"*Fixed windows with wide sills went all around the small room. … A telephone, an open microphone, a flashlight, binoculars, a button to release the security gate on the road below, and an electric heater completed the furnishings. A few feet from the door, an emergency searchlight was mounted on the catwalk.*"

—George Gregory, Correctional Officer

The hospital was run by the US Public Health Service and included a large treatment room, X ray and operating rooms, a psychiatric ward, and several sick rooms. "Birdman" Robert Stroud spent eleven years in this isolation hospital cell before being transferred to the Medical Center for Federal Prisoners in Springfield, Missouri, in 1959.

"*The Control Center was the office for lieutenants and the place where all central control of the custodial force was maintained. It was also the center of communications. No prisoners were allowed in this portion of the building.*"

—Erwin N. Thompson,
Historian, National Park Service

> 21 MARCH 1963
> ASSORTED DRY CEREALS
> STEAMED WHOLE WHEAT
> 1 SCRAMBLED EGGS
> 2 FRESH MILK
> STEWED FRUIT
> TOAST
> BREAD
> BUTTER
>
> COFFEE

Above: **Menu for the inmates' last meal on Alcatraz.**

"Reporters and photographers rambled through cellblocks, tested the sound-proofing in 'solitary,' and inspected the doctor's office."

—*Pittsburgh Press,*
March 22, 1963

"The first women [and children] ever to see the inside of the grim cellblocks wandered along the corridors of the empty tiers. The occasion was the removal of the last 27 inmates imprisoned on Alcatraz ... and the first unrestricted press tour of the island penitentiary."

—*San Francisco News Call Bulletin*, March 21, 1963

An anything-but-ordinary work day ends with a boat ride back to San Francisco.

"*There will always be the need for specialized facilities for the desperados, the irredeemable, and the ruthless, but Alcatraz and all that it had come to mean now belong, we may hope, to history.*"

—James V. Bennett, Director,
US Bureau of Prisons, 1963

ALCATRAZ ISLAND, TEN YEARS LATER
by John Martini, Historian and National Park Service Ranger

The National Park Service opened Alcatraz to the public for the first time in October 1973. The years since the prison closed had not been kind to the Rock.

Beginning in late 1969, the island was the site of a much-publicized occupation by "Indians of All Tribes," mostly Native American students following the tradition of 1960s radical action. After the last occupiers were removed in 1971, the island was put under control of the General Services Administration (GSA), who—fearful of another occupation—undertook the demolition of the remaining habitable structures. Before they were done, GSA wrecking balls demolished another eight Alcatraz buildings in addition to the ones that had burned down during the occupation.

When Alcatraz was turned over to the National Park Service as part of the newly created Golden Gate National Recreation Area, it looked as though urban warfare had been waged across its slopes and through its cellblocks. NPS staff charged with getting it ready for its public opening faced huge challenges in making it safe for life and limb.

To clear a pathway for visitors, they staged marathon sweeping parties and pushed accumulated debris into nearby buildings or onto the vast parade ground. Temporary fences restricted access to the most dangerous parts of the island. You might say that "temporary" was the operative word; prevailing wisdom held that the public would become bored with the island after a few years and it would be put to other uses.

By the time I arrived on Alcatraz as a park ranger a few months later, the island had only been marginally tidied up. Mountains of rubble still stood alongside burned-out concrete shells, and broken glass and trash filled almost every building. The less said about the few intact toilets, the better. Alcatraz was still basically a giant hazard. Someone joked that we should just paint yellow-and-black safety stripes on the whole island.

Modern-day Alcatraz bears little resemblance to the place I saw in 1973. It has become a National Historic Landmark, preserved to tell its stories as a military post, penitentiary, and Native American occupation site. Thanks to ongoing cleanup and preservation efforts, rubble piles have been removed or safely stockpiled, and once-hazardous areas have been cleaned up and opened for visitation. Ruins are now stabilized, the road has been repaired, and gardens once again flourish in the shadow of the prison.

It will never be possible to restore Alcatraz to the way it looked the day the penitentiary closed. Instead, the island will reflect all its historic eras—and its sometimes drastic changes—in keeping with the National Park Service's century-long mission: to protect and preserve for the enjoyment of future generations.

John Martini spent most of his National Park Service career as an interpretive ranger and historian before retiring from the NPS in 1999; he is widely acknowledged as an expert on the island's past.

Frank Sinatra, 1958

LEIGH WIENER
(1929–1993)

Taking remarkable photographs requires much more than proficiency with light meter and lens. It demands an eye for composition, an understanding of human nature, and an almost mystical sixth sense about when to squeeze the shutter. Photographer and photojournalist Leigh Wiener had all of these skills, and more, and used them to create thousands of memorable images over the course of a career that spanned almost five decades.

To Wiener, exceptional photographs weren't accidents of time and place. Nor did he believe in "the decisive moment"; the photographer defined the moment, not vice versa. "As a photographer, you create the image. You decide when to release the shutter. You, the photographer, are the decisive element in the taking of the photograph, not some hyped-up moment. Your sensitivity and your understanding of the subject matter, and your point of view, will determine whether your photograph is decisive or not."

Born and raised in New York City, Wiener was the son of a newspaperman. His early interest in photography was cultivated by family friend Arthur Fellig (AKA "Weegee"), who was famous for his gritty street photography. Fellig was a frequent guest in the Wiener home; when he stopped by for Sunday dinner, he made it a practice to show the young man his most

Leigh Wiener (Undated photo by Mario A. Casilli)

recent photographs and ask his opinion. This visual training paid off when fourteen-year-old Wiener made his first professional sale to Collier's magazine.

In 1946, he moved to Los Angeles. He was working for the *Los Angeles Times* in 1949 when his photograph of an empty swing at the California home of Kathy Fiscus, the three-year-old who fell down a well, ran on the front pages of more than one hundred newspapers across the country.

Wiener went on to establish his own company in 1958, and over the years, produced front-page photos and photo essays for some of the nation's leading newspapers and magazines. From dishwashers, a roller-skating rooster, and

Across left: **The Empty Swing, 1949**; Across right: **Duke Ellington, 1961**; Above left: **Midnight Mission, 1957**; Above right: **Grace Kelly, 1955**

a kimono-clad woman on a Japanese street to presidents, Hollywood legends, musicians, poets, and scientists: he had an omnivorous eye for interesting subjects. Wiener also published nine books featuring his work, and received numerous awards for his football documentary, *A Slice of Sunday*.

The intensity of many of Wiener's remarkable photographs comes not only from their composition but also from the effects he achieved by combining cameras and lenses, and the setups he designed to materialize what he saw in his mind's eye. "In many ways, innovation is a photographer's lifeblood. He has an idea and wants to obtain a cer-

tain look. Just because there is no ready-made equipment available doesn't mean you can't develop the idea. Make it yourself. Sometimes innovation doesn't require special hardware or equipment; it might just involve a different method of lighting or a new technique…. It is no accident that great photographers are also great innovators."

124

In a 1988 interview with the *Los Angeles Times*, Wiener summed up the value of still photography: "Two or three of the most important news stories of this century occurred before live news cameras. ABC, CBS, and NBC had [Lee Harvey] Oswald being shot by [Jack] Ruby, live. It lasted 2.3 seconds. No one knew what happened. They re-ran it and re-ran it and still nobody knew what happened.

"One photographer from the *Dallas Times* [*Herald*] took one still photograph and the world knew what happened. You could look into the eyes of Ruby and Oswald and see the relationship."

Leigh Wiener's photographs are in the permanent collection of the National Portrait Gallery, among others. See more of his work at *www.leighwiener.com*.